Faith in God

FAITH IN GOD

The Unseen Steps to Victory

Lynette Shelto-Johnson

Copyright 2023 The Lynette Shelto-Johnson Book, England 2023

First published 2023

English translation 2023

Lynette Shelto-Johnson has asserted her right under the copyright design to be identified as the author of this book.

This book is sold subject to the condition that it shall not, by way of trade or otherwise, be lent, resold, hired out or otherwise circulated other than in the form in which it is published and without similar conditions, including this condition being imposed on the subsequent purchaser.

Extracts from the authorised version of the Bible (The King James Bible)

ISBNs
978-1-80541-209-0 (paperback)
978-1-80541-210-6 (eBook)

Contents

Preface	vii
Blessings from God	1
Miracles of Life	7
Forgiveness	11
Trials and Strength	15
Hope and Endurance	21
Brokenness and Personal Revival	27
The Love of God	33
Love in the Home	37
A Servant for the Lord	43
The Power of Prayer	51
Faith and Belief	59
Acknowledgements	69
Reasons for Writing this Book	73
Summary	75

Preface

This is the first publication of this book. With the years of experience and the many faith encounters I have experienced with God, you will have the feeling of God's love when you read the contents of this book.

The truths expressed in these pages lie at the heart of all those movements of revival through which God has restored to billions who need his love.

Despite the unprecedented times, God's grace and mercies are glorious memories of the past, and his grace and mercies are still given freely to us today and always.

The pages of this book have a special relevance for the readers today, and I pray and trust that this book may, with the blessings of God, be the means of helping millions to accept God, who is the only help for our existence. The contents of this book will help readers have that Holy Ghost revival through the confession of emptiness and failure.

This book expresses the truth that lies at the heart of faith, hope and personal revival.

I dedicate this book to the memories of my loving mother Yvonne Alice Francis Shelto, my father Vernon Shelto Gillis, my nephew Peter McLennon, my sister Lorraine Shelto as well as other relatives who are no longer with us.

I look forward to the second coming of our Lord and Saviour, Jesus Christ, when this world shall live in perfect peace and love. The new Jerusalem will be delivered by God from heaven. There shall be no more sickness or death, for God shall wipe away all tears from our eyes, and God himself will be our king, and he shall rule and reign forever.

My family and I continue to put God first in our daily lives, and I pray that you too will do the same to put God first in your life.

May God bless us all.

Glory be to God!

Lynette Shelto-Johnson
March 2023

Blessings from God

These are precious and priceless.

Every day we wake up is a beautiful gift from God. Our greatest blessing is our best sacrifice, which is Jesus Christ, our Lord. We must thank God for sending his best gift from the splendour of glory to die for us and save us. His name is Jesus Christ. King of all kings and Lord of all lords.

Burdens were lifted at Calvary through the sacrificial price Christ paid on the cross. He bled and died, so you and I could be free from our sins. Whoever God's son sets free is truly free. When you are set free by the cleansing blood of the Lord, Jesus Christ, your sins will be in the past. You will then be a new person in Christ Jesus. The King James Bible tells us that old things have passed away and old things have become new. The son of God shall set your heart free to worship him in spirit and in truth.

Millions of people pray for blessings when blessings are facing them every day. Each new day, God gives us brand new mercies. His grace is sufficient for you and me.

We wake up; it is a blessing. We can see it is a blessing. We can walk, talk, run and hear. These are all free and priceless blessings. Please do not forget about your children, other families and friends. They are great and priceless blessings. Your jobs. Your houses, cars, etc. These are all blessings from Almighty God. Health, strength, happiness, peace, joy and faith. Our educational status, our successes, our talents. You name it. These are all amazing blessings given to us by God.

We don't exist by accident. Even in a time of great suffering, Job recognised he was created by God for a special purpose. Despite Job's suffering, he still served God.

It is the spirit of God who supplies our every breath, but this is not just the oxygen we draw from the air. The Holy Spirit makes us alive in Christ, freeing us from the spiritual death brought on by sin.

When I look back at the 2020 pandemic with extreme thanks and gratitude to God, I reflect on the fact that millions did not make it, but you and I did. It is a great and priceless blessing from God that we made it through the pandemic only through the grace and mercies of God. Many days I can remember it like it was yesterday. Some of my nurses went off sick, and I had no choice but to close my office and go on the unit to help the other nurses. I cared for patients with COVID-19. Was I afraid? Yes, but I had to give the best possible nursing care I could have given, not forgetting the best infection control measures to prevent cross-contamination. I was thankful to God that I did not lose any staff to COVID-19. I was also thankful to God that I did not have many patient deaths from the virus. I had a small percentage of patient deaths, which affected us emotionally, but we were thankful compared to other health sectors that had numerous deaths from COVID-19. My workplace recovered quickly from the virus with excellent nursing skills, effective infection control guidelines and measures, great teamwork and excellent team spirit, prayers, and God's grace and mercies. We are grateful to God and everyone who played a part in helping. such as doctors and community professionals.

Sometimes I had visitors in my office who asked how we overcame the virus so quickly. My answer to them was that God was the answer. Without God, we couldn't have done it. All praise and thanks to Almighty God.

I am also grateful and thankful to God for my life and the lives of my family, friends and everyone else out there. If it wasn't for the Lord's guidance and protection, none of us would have made it so far.

I contracted COVID-19 in January 2021, and no one else in my home contracted it during that time. I thank God for that too. I thank God that I had no serious complications. My daughter Crystal contracted COVID-19 early in 2022 and again in June 2022, but thank God she too had no serious complications. She was afraid I would catch the virus from her, but thank God I was fine.

My daughter completed law school during the pandemic, and I thought she would not have been able to focus on her studies, but by God's strength, she did get through it. I remember days and nights when, despite the daily government census of thousands of deaths daily from the COVID-19 virus, my daughter Crystal was emotionally sad but still got on with her studies. Only the true and living God could give us victory within the storms of life. The peak of the pandemic was very scary, with serious, unprecedented circumstances and uncertain times, but God was our hope and strength.

My daughter Crystal graduated with a master's degree in law, and she is presently working at a law firm.

You and I have all had so many blessings that we can thank God for, and those blessings will be countless, precious and priceless.

Every breath of air we breathe is a blessing from God. Every step we take is a blessing.

FAITH IN GOD

Each new morning, God grants us new grace and mercies. He is a great, big, wonderful God.

When God blesses us, no one can say no. When God blesses us, no one can take that blessing away but God himself.

Miracles of Life

We should never be discouraged. Take it to the Lord in prayer. God's favour is a gift of grace. God always has a plan for us. So many times we try to succeed with our plan, but God's plan always takes us to victory. Sometimes our own plan fails, but God always has the perfect plan.

One of the greatest miracles was when God raised Jesus from the grave. Millions today are still in doubt, and millions do not believe it is possible, but the true and living God is a god of unspeakable miracles. He is a great, big, wonderful God. A god who can make a desert like a fountain and can calm the raging sea.

Abraham's greatest blessing was when his wife gave him a son at a very old age. Many people were speechless, but that is the God we serve. He is a god of miracles.

FAITH IN GOD

God's greatest gift to us is sending Jesus to die so we can have forgiveness of our sins.

When we were yet sinners, Christ died for us. Our blessings are our children. Our families are our blessings. Our friends. Our jobs. Shelter. Food. Clothing. The gift of life is family and friends. Oh, what amazing miracles of God! The strangers along the way are also great blessings that are added to our lives. Everyone we meet in life has a part to play in God's plan for our lives. It may be for wonderful blessings or a good or painful lesson.

The parting of the Red Sea is one of the greatest and most dramatic stories of Earth's history. With the mighty powers of God invested in Moses, God parted the big, mighty Red Sea. The Israelites crossed the sea on dry ground. This amazing story can be found in the Bible.

Many people pray for miracles, not realising that each new day on planet Earth is a great miracle. The birth of each new baby is a miracle. I heard of people who said they had never seen a miracle and yet they had many children. Little did they realise that all the children they gave birth to were miracles from God. The air we breathe is a miracle and a blessing.

I am not only a registered nurse, but I am also a midwife by profession. I was privileged by God to witness many babies enter this world. It was heart-touching to see their faces and hear their cries as they glided their way out into this beautiful world. Seeing the joy and happiness on the faces of mothers and fathers too was awesome. During my days in midwifery school, I was amazed at the miraculous works of God where conception, pregnancy and delivery are concerned. Everything is in perfect order. This entire process is a great, big, wonderful miracle of God.

I didn't have the chance to hear my daughter cry at birth because I had a caesarean section, and I was knocked out, so to speak. Nevertheless, just the joy of waking up knowing my surgery went well and giving birth to a beautiful, healthy baby girl was a dream came true with unspeakable joy. God is good.

FAITH IN GOD

The gynaecologist said it was not possible, and God said, "Watch me. I am a god of impossibilities."

Glory be to God!

Forgiveness

Many people find it difficult to forgive someone who may have hurt them in some way or another. Many people may not speak to each other. Some people do not speak to their neighbours for one reason or another.

Without forgiveness, there is no remission of sin. If we want God to forgive us of our sins, then we should be able to forgive one another. Holding grudges is a burden to the soul and could bring on emotional and physical trauma. Letting go of grudges and hatred will free your mind from any form of emotional burden. It will give you that inner peace from God. The love of God will help you entertain those feelings of forgiveness. Do not harden your heart from forgiving someone because you may have hatred for them. Allow the love of God to flow in your heart. Eventually, the gift of forgiveness will dominate your heart, soul and mind. You will then have that inner peace to release, let go, free up your mind and forgive.

Forgiveness is a powerful gift from God that will bring happiness into your hearts.

Our calling is between us and God. You and I can make it sure by accepting God. When God blesses us, he wants us to use our blessings to honour him. God wants us to use our blessings to bless others. Don't sit on your blessings. Use your blessings to honour Christ. Use your time, use your talents, use your knowledge and use your wealth to glorify God. When God blesses us, no one can say no.

You may have noticed I named my book *Faith in God: The Unseen Steps to Victory*. Forgiveness is like putting your feet on an unseen step, knowing God is with you to place the next step every time you climb the ladder to victory. Forgiveness is like a miracle. Forgiveness will make you a brand new person in the spiritual realm. Forgiveness purifies your heart, mind and soul. It plunges you into the fountain of love and happiness. Even if you don't have material wealth, forgiveness in and of itself is a great treasure from God. It is profound and priceless. Forgiveness is one of God's powerful tools that he gave to us so we could secure ourselves in his salvation, which is vital for our spiritual revival.

Trials and Strength

The King James Bible teaches us that a time will come when trials and testing will increase. The Bible always tells us about the shaking and shifting times. It mentions the Great Tribulation. Our strength relies on the true and living God to get us through these trying times. The Book of Revelation mentions the end times. When we look around the world, all we can see and hear are increasing earthquakes, flooding and crime. Humanity seems more interested in the glamorous things of this world than in the love of God.

According to my sister Doris, this is a serious time when we should be running for cover under the shadow of the Almighty God. This is a daily plea of my sister as she posts her daily inspirational messages on Facebook.

We should be thinking and asking ourselves the question: Where shall we stand at the coming of the Lord Jesus Christ? Would we be found wanting? Or would we hear, "Well done, thy good and faithful servant, enter the gates of our Lord"?

Let us all continue to pray for each other, asking God for the strength for us to continue to walk the path of God. Let us remember to always keep our eyes fixed on the Lord and prepare to make our calling sure with Almighty God.

The world experienced one of the greatest sudden and dramatic changes in 2020, when the COVID-19 killer virus furiously invaded planet Earth. This was an unprecedented time for the world, with millions of lives lost. I pray God continues to comfort the hearts of those who lost loved ones.

Even though COVID-19 is not so prevalent now, we are still living in uncertain times.

The UK also experienced a drastic change with a new era with the passing of the queen in 2022, which was a sad thing for the UK and the world. The UK now has the reign of a new king, and the UK will have to get used to a king instead of a queen.

Speaking about earthquakes in distant places, Turkey and Syria recently had one of the worst earthquakes in Earth's history. So many thousands of lives were lost. I pray that God grants comfort and inner peace to everyone in Turkey, Syria and the world at large.

I pray that you and your family are trusting God in every situation. I am giving God thanks, praise, honour and glory for keeping me and my family, friends and others safe, and you should do the same every day. The trials will come to make us stumble and fall, but thanks be to God. He has sent his angels to rescue us in many situations we don't even know about. We cannot even walk without God holding our hands. The mountain is too high, and the valley is too wide, but on our knees with prayers, we learn how to stand. I just want to let you know that when the mountain is too high, God is carrying you and me on his shoulders. I am praying for you today to encourage you that when things get a little difficult, God is carrying you because he loves you. He is just a prayer away.

In the book of Romans 12:2, the King James Bible teaches us: "And be not conformed to this world: but be ye transformed by the renewing of your mind, that ye may prove what is that good, and acceptable, and perfect will of God."

The world is on a physical and spiritual battlefield. This is because sin entered the world in the Garden of Eden when Adam and Eve disobeyed God. This is how it will continue and even get worse because end-time prophecies will be fulfilled according to the holy scriptures. A hundred percent peace and love will return to planet Earth at the second coming of the Lord. We are all in the same earthly storm, but we are not all in the same boat. Whatever boat you are sailing through the storm with, please make sure you ask God to be in that boat with you and continue to entertain him as long as you live. You and I can never go through an earthly storm safely without the Lord in our boat. The storm is raging everywhere in the world. People are running to and flow to find peace. I would like to tell you today that you can never find real peace and happiness until you find that personal experience and personal relationship with God.

I would like to encourage you to shine your light continuously and without fail. There are many people who are still in spiritual darkness. People who are depressed, people who are aching from one thing or another, people who are thinking about giving up. Shine your light. Help get those people out of the darkness so they can see the light of God.

I know there is an increase in electricity and gas bills everywhere, which is causing financial difficulties for millions of people. Some people are unable to turn on their lights often. This is a sad situation, but I am mostly referring to the spiritual light, which is more vital for our salvation. The spiritual light will heal the hearts and minds of people. It will help people see love above the material things of this world. It will see hatred as something bad. It will let us love our neighbours as ourselves.

Think about these things.

Hope and Endurance

I know my redeemer lives, and he shall shine forth in the day of the coming of the Lord.

Love is of God, and God himself is love. Love shows up in many languages and many situations. Hope is the assurance of knowing that God's promises are real and sealed.

The walls of Jericho are a typical example of hope for things to come. The army endured marching around the city of Jericho for seven days. The King James Bible tells us the men of God endured the daily march. On the seventh day, they marched around the city seven times. When the walls of Jericho came tumbling down, the men of God knew their hard work had paid off. They knew they had not hoped in vain. God came through for them. All they did was march around the city. Did they use guns? The answer is no. Did they use swords? The answer is no. Through the power of God, all the men did was shout on the seventh day of the march, and the walls of Jericho came tumbling down.

During the COVID-19 pandemic, we were in a position of emotional, mental and physical trauma where money and status didn't matter. Everyone needed the same thing, and that was God's saving grace and mercies. The pandemic is over, I would believe, so things appear to be almost back to the way they were pre-pandemic. It was a really scary time, but God gave us that time so we were able to spend a lot of time with our families at home. I can't say the same for the people who have most of their families abroad.

Nevertheless, I love the saying that rain does not fall forever, and storm clouds always pass over. This is true because it seemed like the pandemic was never going to come to an end, but thank the good Lord it did.

If your faith is very strong where hope is concerned, then you have an amazing gift from God. Let us look at the train that goes through the dark tunnel. Do we throw away our train tickets and jump out of the train? The answer is no. We trust God to get us through the tunnel safely. This is where we would pray and trust God to take us safely from the dark tunnel into the brightness outside the tunnel.

In my first book, I wrote about two encounters I had on planes. In both encounters, it was difficult for the planes to land. As far as I can remember, no one tried to jump from the planes because that would have been disastrous. We all sat on the planes in fear, praying and trusting God to take us to our destination safely. We were hoping and praying for God's mercy to land the planes safely. Endurance in faith is greatly required in perilous times because people can become greatly emotionally and physically traumatised if their faith and hoping abilities are weak. Those of us who believe in the coming of the Lord exercise great faith and hope, which blend with patience and endurance. These four gifts from God have to be persistent. The King James Bible mentions the patience of the saints. If you believe in the real and sealed promises of the Lord, you need to continue to cast your eyes on the path and righteousness of God. Let the glamorous things of this world be secondary where the things of God are concerned. The will of God shall prevail, and the writing of his holy word shall be fulfilled.

I love the song that says, "From the valley, I will cast my eyes up to the one who sees me there. From the mountain, I will look to the one who took me there." I named my first book *From the Valley to the Mountain: Blessings and Lessons*. That book is very important to me because it highlighted my struggles when I was down in the valley. It highlighted my successes and struggles as I climbed the mountain of life. In the valley, I was giving God praise and thanks on my good and not-so-good days. During my climb to success, despite some difficult struggles, I continued with my service to Almighty God. I have acquired more than what I prayed for, and this is what I call blessings with overflow. When God blesses us, we should share our blessings with others by either helping others or by telling others about his goodness. This is another reason why I have decided to write. I know this is another way of telling people about the goodness of God.

We will face many defeats in life, but never let yourself be defeated. Rejoice in hope. Endure through tribulations and continue to persevere in prayer. Prayer is powerful and works wonders.

The blood of Jesus washes you and me. The blood of Jesus is our victory. Press forwards to the mark of the calling in Christ Jesus. The Bible didn't tell us to press backwards. Our Bible tells us to press forwards. The soldiers don't cover their backs when they are going to war. They cover the front of their bodies from flying bullets. This is because they are moving forwards towards the enemies.

We should not look back at our mistakes, but rather look forwards with hope and faith in God. There is grace for whatever happened yesterday. There is hope for what happens tomorrow. Stay hopeful. You may not know what tomorrow may bring.

FAITH IN GOD

Always try to think positively about the future. Pray and don't allow negative thoughts to creep into your mind. Promote thoughts filled with hope. Reject any thoughts of negativity. Stay hopeful and don't think that what happened in the past will happen again. Look back at the past with less anxiety knowing God holds your future. Demonstrate gratitude and give thanks to God for your life. When you are stressed out or having feelings of depression, change your daily routine. Visit new environments and attach yourself to things you like to do. Try to treat yourself to nice things. Try to be around people who will motivate your well-being. Try to spend more time enhancing your health and eating well. Dress your best and smile at the world; it will help you feel good about yourself.

Try to invite some family and friends over for dinner. Laugh, chat, speak about old times. Watch a movie if you feel like doing so. Invite a friend to go to church with you. It may be a concert or a picnic, but find things to motivate your heart and mind.

Brokenness and Personal Revival

The first thing you should have for personal revival and personal recovery is the willpower to believe in yourself and believe in God. When God revives us, he instils his love in our hearts. Jesus Christ was victorious at the cross of Calvary.

The same God that holds the world up in his hands is the same God who holds us up when we are broken. God is the greatest mender of broken hearts and broken dreams. He can restore joy to our hearts instantly.

The power of God is matchless, so when you are set free by the power of God, you are indeed free. To heal from brokenness, we need to have that close inner relationship with God to heal our hearts and minds from anything that may make us feel broken. Once you develop that closeness with God, you will see his power being demonstrated in a mighty way in our hearts, our homes, our lives and our service. The victorious life of God will fill us, overflow in us and flow to others. This is what personal revival is, and it can truly make you happy and make others happy. With personal revival, we must learn to put ourselves aside and let the will of God rule our lives. We cannot overcome brokenness if we put ourselves before the will of God.

Falling doesn't define us. The way we rise above our imperfections is what defines us. Smile at the world even if it doesn't smile back at you.

To be broken or to fall is painful, but it is not the falling that is important. It is the way we rise to victory. It is the way we rise to revive ourselves. We can do so with a victorious outcome with God holding our hands. Give God a chance in your life. You shall have no regrets.

Your brokenness will be painful, but your revival will be victorious by the grace of God. The Bible tells us (not I, but Christ).

I know many people ask God to direct their paths, but in fact some people are refusing to move their feet to follow his guidance.

I am aware I already spoke about forgiveness, but forgiveness is also a powerful weapon God gave us to use to heal brokenness and recover from brokenness. It is a great stepping stone to personal revival or personal recovery.

Millions have asked God for forgiveness, yet they hold grudges and refuse to forgive others. For those who do that, their brokenness will get worse, and their personal revival and personal recovery will be delayed. You wouldn't want God to send his son back to Earth and meet you with unforgiveness in your heart, would you? I guess not. The Holy Ghost will not want to live in an unforgiving heart.

When we experience a personal revival with God, that is when we begin to have the overflowing of the Holy Spirit.

Once we have that close relationship with God, we will know we have been revived from brokenness. We will experience that inner peace and the love of God.

In three short months, just like he did with the plagues of Egypt, God took away everything most of the world worships. God said, "You want to worship athletes? I will shut down the stadiums. You want to worship musicians? I will shut down civic centres. You want to worship actors? I will shut down theatres. You want to worship money? I will shut down the economy and collapse the stock market. You don't want to go to church and worship me? I will make it so you can't go to church." This is what happened during the COVID-19 pandemic. It was really unprecedented times with great uncertainties.

"If my people, which are called by my name, will humble themselves, and pray, and seek my face, and turn from their wicked ways; then I will hear from heaven, and will forgive their sin, and will heal their land." (2 Chronicles 7:14) This is a portion of the holy word from the King James Bible.

Maybe we didn't need a vaccine. Maybe we needed that time of isolation from the distractions of the world and a personal revival where we focused on the only thing in the world that really matters: Jesus.

If you believe this, please start the revival in your home. Spread the love of Jesus.

One of the most important and powerful gifts from God is forgiveness. This will help anyone with brokenness and the road to personal revival. God is our strength and power. He makes our way perfect. It is you and I who sometimes stray from the path of God.

God has not given us a spirit of fear but one of power, love and a sound mind. Live every moment, laugh every day and love beyond measure.

Giving up is not an option. Look at the dark clouds. When they blow away, you will see the silver lining.

Today I want to let you know that God is real. If you feel lost and broken, please try praying to the Lord. Believe in him for your personal revival. Believe in God for your personal recovery. Trust in the Lord to take you through the road to personal revival. He will come through for you.

If we think about the reasons for most people's brokenness, it will all add up to the fact we don't allow the Holy Spirit to be fully present in our lives. As a result, when difficult situations face us, our faith and strength in God are not strong enough to endure whatever the problem is. God wants us to obtain the fullness of the Holy Spirit so we can have faith and strength to overcome our problems with his peace and love. We need spiritual growth to overcome brokenness faster, which will lead to personal revival faster before things go downhill. You can listen to people who have experienced brokenness. They might tell you how they were able to overcome such difficult times. Everyone has their own life experience of some form of emotional brokenness, but something from another person's experience might be able to help you make a start on your road to personal recovery.

The Love of God

The love of God is beyond measure. He created us, he sustains us and his grace and mercies are new each morning. God's love is so strong for us he continues to provide for and love those who do not even believe he exists. He continues to demonstrate his love for us. Even those who do not like him, he still loves them all.

The King James Bible teaches us God so loved the world that he gave his only begotten son so that whosoever believes in him shall not perish but have everlasting life.

The son of God left the splendour of heaven to come to this sin-sick earth to die for you and me. Sometimes you may not have food to eat, then suddenly someone gives you something to eat. That is God's love in action. Sometimes your purse or wallet might be empty. Soon afterwards, someone might give you some money. Have you ever told someone they are a godsend? Well, that is God's love in action. God works in various ways to demonstrate his love for us. We see it as people helping us, but God is love, and love is of God. He can use anyone to show his love and share his blessings with us.

Where God is concerned, his love does not have colour. He loves us all with an everlasting love. Let us all strive to make this world a better place where love can triumph and everyone can live as one in unity, love and peace.

Love knows no colour. Love is of God, and love is God. The Guyanese motto is: "One people. One nation. One destiny." Indeed, where God is concerned, we are one in his sight. This is why the garden of many colours is so beautiful. Despite our various colours, we were all created beautiful and were wonderfully made by an awesome God. He loves us with an everlasting love.

It is a powerful thing when you can show love to others even though you may be hurting. In the King James Bible, it says Jesus was on the cross when he showed love to the thief on the cross. He knew the man was a thief, but he showed compassion by saying to the man, "Today you shall be with me in paradise." Those were comforting words to the man on the cross who knew he was going to die.

In the book of John 1, the King James Bible tells us, "In the beginning was the Word, and the Word was with God, and the Word was God." It went on to say the word dwelled amongst men on earth.

God loves us, he loves himself and that love is with us. God loves us unconditionally.

Love in the Home

There is a saying that charity begins at home.

A home will malfunction if God is not in the centre of that home. God should be first in every home setting and any other setting. God is love, and once love is in our homes, the light of God will shine through them. This light of God will shine through us, and others will see the light of God within us. The King James Bible tells us, "Let your light so shine before all men, that they may see your good works, and glorify your Father which is in heaven." (Matthew 5:16)

Parents should teach their children about the love of God in the home. As a result, the children will take the love of God to school and everywhere they go. There are millions of people who are still in spiritual darkness. Let us who have the light of God shine our lights so those who are in darkness may see the light of God within us. The light we shine will help people walk from darkness into God's marvellous light.

I read Michelle Obama's book, *The Light We Carry*, about overcoming uncertain times. It is a beautiful book. Indeed, we carry that light within, and only we alone, by the grace of God, can shine that light. The love we show and share with others is a powerful light we carry, and we may be saving many people from darkness unknowingly. So, please let us continue to show love in our homes and everywhere we go.

I mention later in my book that morning devotions should pave the day for every home. I know that, in this new society, many people are so taken up with the glamorous things of the world that there isn't much time for morning devotions, but the home is in great need of prayers and worship. Most schools have stopped praying before starting the day. It may be why some children are abusive to teachers and some teachers are abusive to children because morning worship to God was taken away from most of the schools.

Parents need to show their children love, and the same goes for the children, who need to show their parents love. Families are precious and priceless gifts given by God. Show them love. Parents, find time for your children. Teach them the path of God so they will remember the teachings in their hearts. Children should find time for their parents, as they will not be there forever.

If your children reach the age of eighteen and they do not want to go and worship God despite your pleas, let prayer be your daily hope. God will be the answer. Trust him for your children's and other families' revival. If children obey the commandment of God to honour their father and mother, there will be a better family relationship in the home.

In times past, God used to be the centre of the home for millions of families. The world needs that again. Schools and every organisation used to welcome God before starting the day. The early church bells used to ring for the morning devotions. The families' devotions used to ring through the air with songs of praise to Almighty God.

A home where God was welcome.

This is a home where God is placed first in everything. With God in our homes, it will be a happy home. A home with peace and love This is a home where God is more important than money. Our strength comes from God.

This is a home where everyone shows unconditional love. The only security we have in faith is in God. There certainly is not anything except the certainty in God. A home where people always thought of their neighbours' welfare and helped where possible. Without contact with God in our homes, our churches, our schools, our workplaces and our hearts, things will never go God's way. A home with godly parents looks out for their children, teaches them the way of God and lives by example. The world needs to go back to the ways of God before time changes into eternity. The probation door will soon close, and souls will be lost from gaining salvation. Perilous times are upon us. The shaking and shifting times are upon us. Tribulation times are upon us.

Can we serve two masters at the same time? Definitely not. Choose this day whom you may serve. God loves us all with an everlasting love.

Family love is precious and priceless. When in danger, such as during the pandemic, everyone thinks about their families. Family is the first thing that comes to mind when it comes to Christmas. Everyone wants to be with their families. Everyone wants to hug loved ones and enjoy the warm environment of the family circle. This is why it is vital that God be at the centre of our homes. God had a plan for humans when he created this world, so families are a very important part of society. Family love will grow if we put God first in everything we do. God wanted love in the family, but because of sin, things don't always go as planned in the family circle. In today's world, there are lots of broken homes, broken marriages, broken relationships, broken dreams and much more. There is no such thing as a perfect family, but some families are coping better because God is welcome in their home.

Despite all of the chaos and confusion in many families, I would like to remind you that Jesus is the deliverer, and he is the answer to life's situations.

With God at the centre of the home, love, strength and unity will prevail.

A Servant for the Lord

Before Jesus left the splendour of glory, he had the heavenly host of angels who were his servants. When he walked the earth, the disciples were his servants and those who followed him. When Jesus was about to return to his heavenly father, he told his disciples to go and make men fishers of men. He told them to go and save men and women for the kingdom of God. Today, we are all servants for God. Let us demonstrate the love of God to everyone we meet. Let us tell everyone about the good news of God's salvation plan. It doesn't matter what you want, but God's plan must come first. Some people are ashamed of sharing the gospel of Christ. The Bible tells us that if we deny God, he will deny us when he comes in glory.

Most of the time, we are busy, but we need to find time to do the work of God. God has called all of us to work for him. This could be so many things. You can give a smile to someone along the way. You can help your neighbours in need. You can tell people about the love of God. You can help someone at work or you can help a stranger. You can live your life in a good way for others to see, so they too can see the good light in you, and they too can do the same.

Continue to shine your light. Continue to be a beacon for the Lord. Lost souls will see your light and be able to walk from darkness into the light of God. Sharing the word of God is another way you and I can tell people about the goodness of God. As for me, writing this book is another way I have chosen to spread the message about the goodness of God. I preached in church for the Women's Ministry Day, and my message was entitled "Faith in God". Everyone was touched by the message that God instilled in me to administer that day to his people. My message only touched the hearts of the people at my church, so I have decided to write this book because I know it will circulate more and bless the hearts of many more people. This message will inspire many people, so they too will be blessed with the message about faith in God.

Despite the perilous times and the difficult tasks at work, I find the time to speak to my staff, my patients and visiting professionals. There were times when I could see a member of staff may be going through a silent battle, and I would call that person in for a chat. I usually blend my conversation with a message of faith and hope. Ninety-five percent of the time, people leave my office with a smile because the word of God and the comforting peace and love of God through me brought deliverance to his people. I know many of you can attest to helping people in this manner. If you do, keep doing that because we are in a spiritual battlefield on Earth. We are living in uncertain times. We are living in perilous times where only the love of God will be able to carry us through the tribulation times.

There may be times when people say hurtful things to you. Stay calm, give them a smile, say a nice word if you may and look at the outcome. Their attitude towards you will eventually change. They may thank you in the end because it is not about what was said. It is about your response. Stay on the path of love. Live love in your home and everywhere you go. Share love. Show love. Teach love. Live every moment. Laugh every day and love beyond measure.

"Blessed is he that cometh in the name of the Lord." (Matthew 21:9)

In the book of John 1 in the King James Bible, it tells us that, "In the beginning was the Word, and the Word was with God, and the Word was God." The Bible went on to say that the word walked no earth and dwelled amongst men. That word that dwells amongst men was Jesus, and he remains the same everlasting Lord.

You and I should be willing to do some good deed every day for others. This will help to brighten the lives of those with whom we share our blessings.

Someone may be in deep darkness, and your good deed may bring them from that place of darkness into some form of emotional comfort and happiness.

Some people believe we can only have the Holy Spirit if we speak in tongues. Speaking in tongues is a special gift from God. I believe once we believe and accept the Lord in our lives, walk with God, do his will and believe in his promises, the Holy Spirit will live within us. The Holy Spirit should be with us all the time and not only when we speak in tongues. During worship, God allows some people to speak in tongues. Not everyone is given that gift from God.

Sometimes people do a lot of things against God, which causes the Holy Spirit to grieve.

Sustaining the Holy Spirit in our lives is when we have that daily communion with God and allow God to dwell in our lives. This is when we walk the way of God, do the will of God and obey his will. Once we continue to allow God to direct our path and move our feet to his guidance, we stand a chance of making our calling sure at the coming of our Lord and Saviour, Jesus Christ. The same Holy Spirit who lives in Christ Jesus also lives in us. We can do all things through Christ Jesus, who gives us strength. God the father, God the son, and God the Holy Spirit.

"In the beginning was the Word and the Word was with God, and the Word was God." This portion of scripture can be found in the book of John 1.

Jesus is the deliverer of mankind. Even Mary, who was handpicked to give birth to him, didn't understand at first what was going on, but the angels of the Lord said fear not, he shall save the world from sin.

It is true that this world is not our own as we are all passing through. Only the work we do for God and the love of God will save us. Sometimes we may feel alone, but God is always with us to love us and motivate us.

Many of us may try to please everyone a hundred percent, but that is impossible. You may do ninety-eight percent of the right things, but people will only notice the two percent that are incorrect. Be encouraged. You may give and not receive. Be encouraged. You may love and not receive love in return. Be encouraged. You may be kind, but people may be unkind to you. Be encouraged. The joy and love of God are our strength.

Never say someone is cold because you don't know what they are going through. Never assume someone is happy because of a smile that may not be real.

Let us try this year to look out for each other and strangers who may need our emotional and physical support. Remember to look out for your neighbours. Show them love and kindness. Remember, even if you give and don't receive, God will still bless you in abundance.

I sometimes feel the same, but I realise that the more I give, the more God blesses me in return. Then again, in life, not everyone you bless will bless you back. Strangers will bless you out of nowhere because God will not approach you in physical form, but he will send someone.

Be encouraged. Be motivated. Be determined to share the love of God, despite the way people may treat you. When people may be unkind, you may feel unloved sometimes. God loves you and me unconditionally. We may have families and friends who show conditional love, but God's love for us is unconditional. He is a great, big, wonderful God.

This is a year that God has already blessed. Let's pray and trust God that whatever this year holds for us, God's will will prevail. May our heart's desires be accomplished through Jesus' name. Amen.

The Power of Prayer

Praying is one of the best weapons God gave us to protect ourselves spiritually, emotionally and physically. Prayer is a powerful gift that helps us communicate with God in the spiritual realm. Praying to God gives us the inner peace of knowing he hears us when we pray. God always answers prayers. It may not always be the answers we want to receive, but God sees ahead and he knows what is best for us. God likes it when we use prayers to communicate with him. Sometimes he delays answering our prayers. Sometimes he answers right away, and sometimes he does not answer our prayers, but he takes our prayers and answers them on a higher level. Many of us were given more than what we prayed for. When you don't get an answer to your prayers, keep praying and keep trusting God. He will answer your prayers in his own way, in perfect timing. He will come through for you.

Prayers can move mountains. Prayers can work wonders through the power of Almighty God. Exercise faith and trust in God when you pray. Believe that God will answer your prayers.

Try to cultivate a habit of praying in your home. If you are going to a school that does not pray before the lesson starts, you can still offer a word of prayer to God before the lesson starts. It should be the same when you go to work. Pray before you start your working day. Do not forget to pray before leaving your home. Ask God for protection and guidance, especially those who are driving. Ask God to be your eyes and ears as some folks drink and drive.

I lost one of my nephews, Peter McLennon, to a drunken driver. His life was taken away suddenly at a young age. I always plead with drivers to take caution and not drink and drive. Please let your passengers get to their destination alive. Take caution on the highway, and please don't speed.

My father used to say, "When you drive, let your eyes be for yourself and the other drivers too." Focus everywhere as a child might suddenly run out on the road.

Prayers help you pass your exams. Prayers help you to be healed in Jesus' name emotionally, physically and spiritually. Many people who were suffering from addiction were healed through the power of prayer.

I went through lots of difficult situations, but faith in God, trust and prayers got me through those difficult times.

I remember during my nursing school days, the director never allowed us to start the class day without praying and singing. It was a difficult, compact three years of training, but the power of daily prayers through Almighty God got us through.

Prayer is powerful. It is one of the most powerful tools God gave us to communicate our needs to him. In the King James Bible, there are so many prayer examples we can look at. Let us use Moses as an example.

Moses was a hard-working man. He went through at least three different careers. He was the privileged ruler in Egypt, the forgotten shepherd in Midian, and the national liberator and leader of the Israelites. Throughout these pursuits, Moses regularly turned to God in prayer.

He debated with God about his fitness to lead Israel out of Egypt. He intercedes on behalf of the Egyptians. He asked for water for his thirsty nation of refugees. He pleaded with God about the sinful Hebrews and what God would do to them. He intercedes with God concerning his sister's leprosy after she exhibited prejudice against Moses' foreign-born spouse. He prayed for the transition of leadership to Joshua. He appealed to God to allow him to join his people in their entrance to the Promised Land. The Bible tells us God told Moses he would see the Promised Land from afar, but he would not enter.

According to the Bible (Deuteronomy), Moses ascended Mount Nebo in the land of

Moab (today's Jordan), and from there he saw the land of Canaan (the Promised Land), which God said he would not enter. Moses then died there at 120 years old.

Joshua led the Israelites into the Promised Land with the guidance of God.

How would you feel if you did so much for the work of God and yet everyone was able to enter that Promised Land except you? Well, Moses wanted to enter the Promised Land, but he did as God instructed and saw the land from afar.

Moses demonstrated the often-forgotten truth that God is more than ready to hear our complaints, appeals and frustrations. You and I too can approach God in prayer about the problems we have.

> "Lord, prepare me to be a sanctuary
> Pure and holy, tried and true
> And with thanksgiving I'll be a living sanctuary
> Oh for You"

FAITH IN GOD

God is calling us to worship him in spirit and in truth. God is calling us back to the altar of worship. God is calling us back to family morning worship and family evening worship. God is calling us back to prayer meetings. God is calling us back to community visitations. God is calling us back to open our classrooms with worship. God is calling us back to open our daily chores with morning devotions.

God is calling the men back to lead the family in morning devotions. God is calling us back to loving our neighbours as ourselves. God is calling us back to share our goods with those in need. God is calling us back to look out for each other and let our community be like a family. God is calling us back to respect the altar of God, and let us remember that, despite the perilous times, God is still on his throne. Amen.

Family and friends, let us pray for each other. Let us pray for our children, family, friends and others who have strayed from the pastures of the living God. It is a sad thing when we are in worship and some of our children, families and friends are elsewhere and not on the path of God. The glamorous things of this world are turning many people from the path of God, but the things of this world will grow strangely dim in the light of God's glory and grace. Tribulation times are upon us. Which side will you be on when the son of God returns? Think about these things. We cannot serve God and man at the same time. Choose this day whom you will serve. I just want to remind us all that prayer changes things and that nothing is impossible with God. I pray God will pour out his holy revival on our land and save us all from now on into eternity. The probation door will close, and I pray all of us will be saved in the kingdom of God.

Let the words of my mouth and the meditation of my heart be acceptable in your sight, O Lord, my strength and redeemer. Amen.

Faith and Belief

"Now faith is the substance of things hoped for, the evidence of things not seen." This is a portion of Bible text you can read in the book of Hebrews 11:1. This is a beautiful message from the King James Bible just to remind you that faith makes things possible, not easy.

Sometimes we do not have strong faith, so when we pray and ask God for things, we doubt him. You and I need to continue trusting that God will grant us the desires of our hearts according to his will.

I love the song that says faith in God can move a mighty mountain. One of my favourite songs is the one I sang in the choir for the Women's Ministry Day, and we also sang this song at a church concert. It went on to say that faith can calm the troubled seas. Faith can make the desert like a fountain. What a beautiful song and what an awesome God we serve.

I don't know about tomorrow, but I know who holds tomorrow and I know who holds my hands.

I was brought up in a God-fearing home where gospel morning devotions paved the start of the day. I am a true believer and worshipper of God. My faith in God became stronger due to some sudden changes in my family life. In July 2011, one of my nephews, Peter McLennon, was taken suddenly from this world due to a speeding bus accident in Guyana, which claimed the lives of five people. The death of my nephew reminded me there is uncertainty in the lives of everyone. This drew me closer to God.

The second life-changing experience for me was when the doctor told my mom the pain in her side was due to muscle pain from the stroke she had previously suffered. Weeks later, my mom was diagnosed with cancer and was given eighteen months to live. My mother lived for two years after the diagnosis, and she passed on 12 March 2012.

FAITH AND BELIEF

This made me more conscious of how uncertain life is, and I realised we all have to die someday. I believe God's promises are real and sealed, and there must be a better world out there. I have faith in the promises of God. My faith in God is strong, without doubt, because I had a close faith experience with him. This was when the gynaecologist told me I wouldn't be able to conceive, but faith in God caused me to conceive and give birth to my daughter, who is now twenty-six years old and has completed law school.

What an awesome God we serve!

I mentioned some faith stories in my sermon in church for the Women's Ministry Day on 4 March 2023. I stopped halfway through my message to ask the choir to join me in singing that faith in God can move a mighty mountain.

I went on to speak about the faith story of Moses and the Israelites at the great, big Red Sea. The amazing works of God with the pillar of fire and the strong wind to stop the Egyptians failed because the pharaoh's heart was hardened.

FAITH IN GOD

One of the greatest faith stories is when the Israelites crossed the Red Sea on dry ground. I am so fearful that I would have been afraid to cross, thinking about the water on both sides of the ocean. As I am older and wiser now, I have faith and trust in Almighty God, and I believe our redeemer lives, and he shall save us on the day of judgement once we stay on the side of the Lord.

One of the other faith stories was the story of the walls of Jericho. The men of God only had to shout around the walls of Jericho to conquer the enemies. They did not use bullets or swords. All they did was march around the city of Jericho for seven days, and on the seventh day, they marched around the city seven times. And on the seventh time, on the seventh day, they gave loud shouts, and the walls of Jericho came down. These were instructions given by God, and the men followed the instructions of God.

Without faith, it is impossible to please God. Belief and faith work together to increase hope and assurance. The story of Moses and the walls of Jericho can be seen in the Bible.

FAITH AND BELIEF

I remember seeing a movie in the 1990s. The movie came out in 1992. The name of the movie is *Leap of Faith*. Those of you who are around my age and the older folks may remember that movie. There were some men and two ladies, I believe. They were travelling from state to state, holding church crusades. They weren't Christians or pastors, but they told the people they were. On the last crusade, those men witnessed a child get up from his wheelchair and walk, but he couldn't walk. Those men were so shocked and amazed that they too were touched by the Holy Spirit that night. They witnessed lots of people being healed before their eyes, and they knew they couldn't have done it. They indeed realised the worshippers were serving the true God as miracles unfolded before their eyes.

This is a fictitious movie, but in real life, it changed the lives of millions of people in such situations. This is an older film, but it's still worth seeing if you enjoy watching movies.

I had to go to the Guyana National Service along with other nurses before we entered the nursing school. It was a requirement in those days. Eight of us were told that if we didn't go to the drill square on our church day, we wouldn't complete the training. On the day of the drill, we stayed in the dorms and worshipped. We were sent to go to the office as a matter of urgency. We were prepared to leave if it came to that. I told the other nurses that God would deliver us just as he delivered the three Hebrew boys from the fiery furnace.

When we arrived at the office, instead of a letter, we were given a big room to worship in. That was so shocking and disbelieving, but then we remembered the God we serve is an awesome God. The captain joined us in service for a few minutes and gave us some snacks. God is good. We all graduated in a guard of honour parade. This is non-fiction. The story of my life.

When I was thirty-two years old, the gynaecologist told me I may not be able to have a child as I had miscarried three times. He also said I waited too long to have children. One year later, I gave birth to my beautiful daughter. She is now twenty-six years old, graduated from law school in 2022, and is now working at a law firm. God is good.

I knew then that women were still giving birth in their forties, so I knew it was still possible for me at age thirty-two. I didn't give up because giving up wasn't an option for me when I knew my redeemer lived. He came through for me.

Whatever you are going through today is preparation, not punishment. There is light at the end of every tunnel.

"For we which have believed do enter that rest." (Hebrews 4:3)

Whenever you're waiting for something to change, perhaps for your health or finances to improve, once you believe, you don't have to figure everything out. When you don't see anything changing, you'll be tempted to worry, but stay calm. When you are at rest, you show God that you trust him. Maybe you are thinking it should have happened by now. You could be worried and complaining, but instead you're thanking God, declaring his promises and doing your best each day. When you're at rest, you're in faith. That's what allows God

FAITH IN GOD

to work. But if you're upset over what's not changing, worried about your finances and can't sleep because your child is off course, that's a sign you've stopped believing. You need to enter into God's rest. Come back to a place of peace. You can't trust God and be worried at the same time. When you're at rest, you know God is in control, you know all things are going to work for your good and you know what he started, he's going to finish.

Here is a prayer for today:

> Father, thank you for providing a place where I can rest in your grace and strength to fight my battles. Thank you that I can stay in peace and know that you will make things happen that I never could. I believe that you are in control and that you'll work it all out for the best. In Jesus' name. Amen.

Now faith is the substance of things hoped for, the evidence of things not seen. For by it, the elders obtained a good report. Through faith, we understand that the worlds were framed by the word of God, so that things which are seen were not made of things which do appear.

By faith, Abel offered unto God a more excellent sacrifice than Cain, by which he obtained witness that he was righteous, God testifying of his gifts: and by it he being dead yet speaketh.

By faith, Enoch was translated that he should not see death; and was not found, because God had translated him: for before his translation he had this testimony, that he pleased God.

But without faith, it is impossible to please him: for he that cometh to God must believe that he is, and that he is a rewarder of those that diligently seek him.

FAITH IN GOD

By faith, Noah, being warned by God of things not seen as yet, moved with fear, prepared an ark for the saving of his house; by which he condemned the world and became the heir of righteousness, which is by faith. (Hebrews 11:1–7)

Acknowledgements

First, I would like to thank Almighty God for the privilege of his grace and mercies in allowing me to write this amazing book to glorify his marvellous name. I want to thank Almighty God for making my first book and this second book a success. I give all praise and thanks to Almighty God.

Secondly, I would like to say thanks to my beautiful and wonderful daughter, who suggested I write a book of inspiration. According to my daughter Crystal, "Mom, you are always encouraging people, and you are always writing these lovely inspiring messages on Facebook." She then said, "Why don't you write a book?" As you can see, I took her suggestion. Glory be to God!

FAITH IN GOD

I preached a sermon in church on 4 March 2023. This was Women's Ministry Day. The message was about faith in God. Everyone said it was a beautiful and inspiring message. This was when my daughter Crystal reminded me again that I should write a book to inspire people. This is why I based my book title on my faith in God.

Thanks to the pastors of my church, the church elders and the church members as they were all supportive towards my message in church and they usually encouraged me by giving me feedback from the messages I wrote on the church group page and other social media. Thanks also to everyone who supported my ministry through my message on the Cross page.

Thanks to my entire family circle, who were always supportive and encouraging of my zest for helping to make the world a better place where love can triumph.

Thanks to all of my friends and families who were supportive with my daily Facebook messages, Instagram messages and the

ACKNOWLEDGEMENTS

messages on my religious page (The Message of the Cross).

Thanks to everyone who supported my first book, *The Valley to the Mountain: Blessings and Lessons*. I do appreciate it so much, and I am truly grateful. I look forward to your continuing support, and I thank you in advance for your support with this book.

Special thanks to the publishing team, Publishing Push: my best and favourite publishing team. I am truly blessed by God to have been given this team to publish my first book and this book. I am pleased with the work done on my books. This publishing team has fully demonstrated and excelled by showing professional excellence. Throughout the entire publishing process, the communication skills and feedback skills were amazing. Thanks to Patrick, Benjamin, Holly and all the other amazing people at Publishing Push Ltd. Well done, everyone! You should be proud of yourselves.

Special thanks also to all the marketing team, the distributors and the workers who deliver the books to various places.

Thanks to everyone who purchased my first book. Thanks also to those of you I have never met. I look forward to your continued support with this book.

I choose Christ when everything around me says to give up. I choose faith and hope. I choose to trust because I believe he is good. He will come through like he said he would.

May God bless you all.

Reasons for Writing this Book

I have a love for writing inspirational messages. I love motivating and counselling people.

I thought if I wrote my inspirational and motivating messages and stories, they would not only inspire people I know but also those who I don't know through the marketing of this book.

I also would like for people to be reminded that, despite what goes on in their lives, God is still on his throne, and he is still in control. I would also like to remind people that God is their strength, provider and sustainer.

Summary

Let us all strive to make this world a better place where love can triumph and everyone can live as one in unity, love and peace.

Love knows no colour. Love is of God, and love is God. The Guyanese motto is: "One people. One nation. One destiny." Indeed, where God is concerned, we are one in his sight. We are one in the spirit of God. This is why the garden of many colours is so beautiful. Despite our various colours, we were all created beautiful and were wonderfully made by an awesome God. He loves us with an everlasting love.

May God bless us all. Glory be to God.

www.ingramcontent.com/pod-product-compliance
Lightning Source LLC
Chambersburg PA
CBHW021121080526
44587CB00010B/595